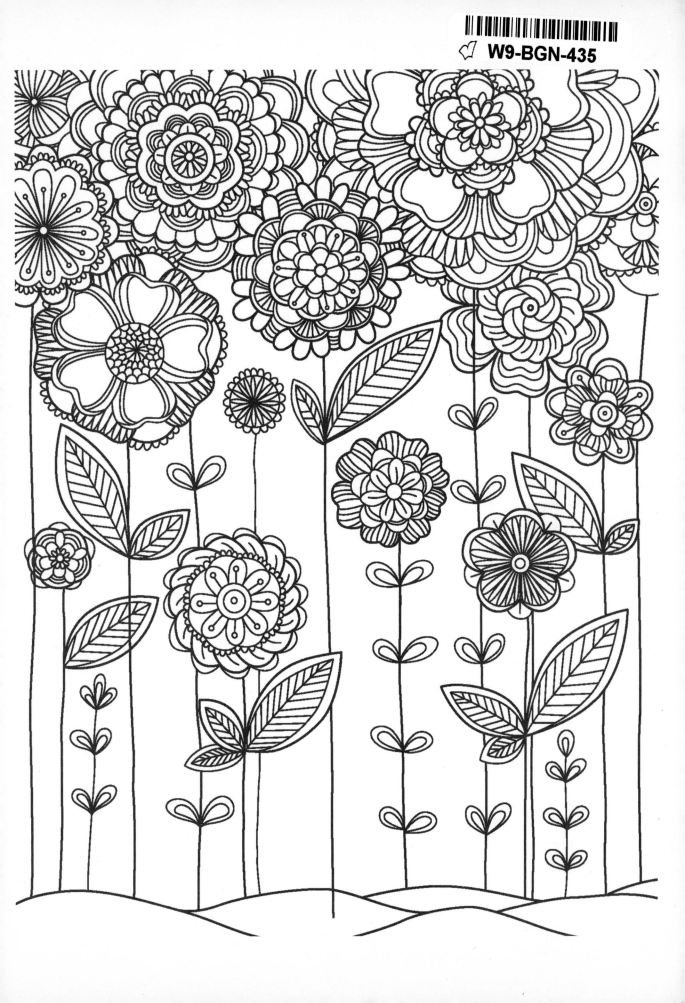

LET YOUR STORY FLOURISH

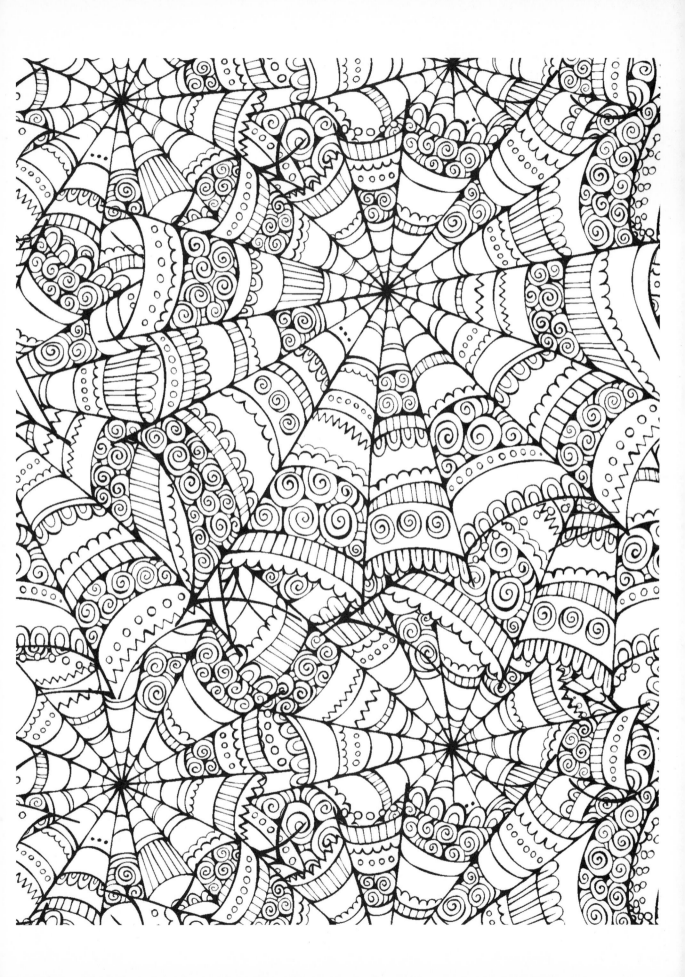

I UNTANGLE MY WORRIES BY...

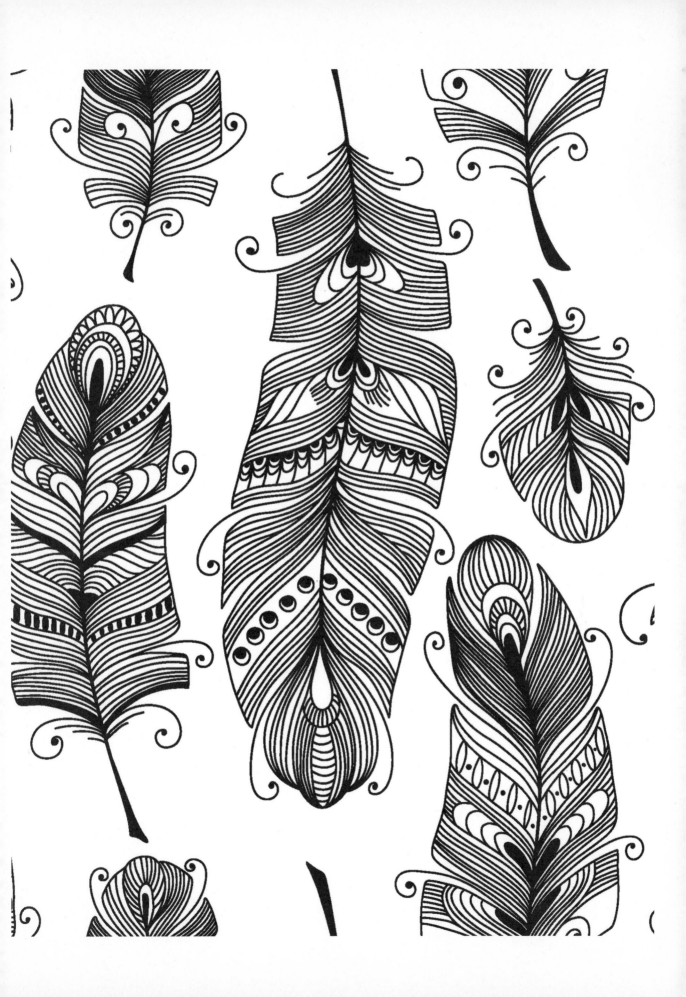

LIGHT AS A FEATHER, MY THOUGHTS FLOW FREELY

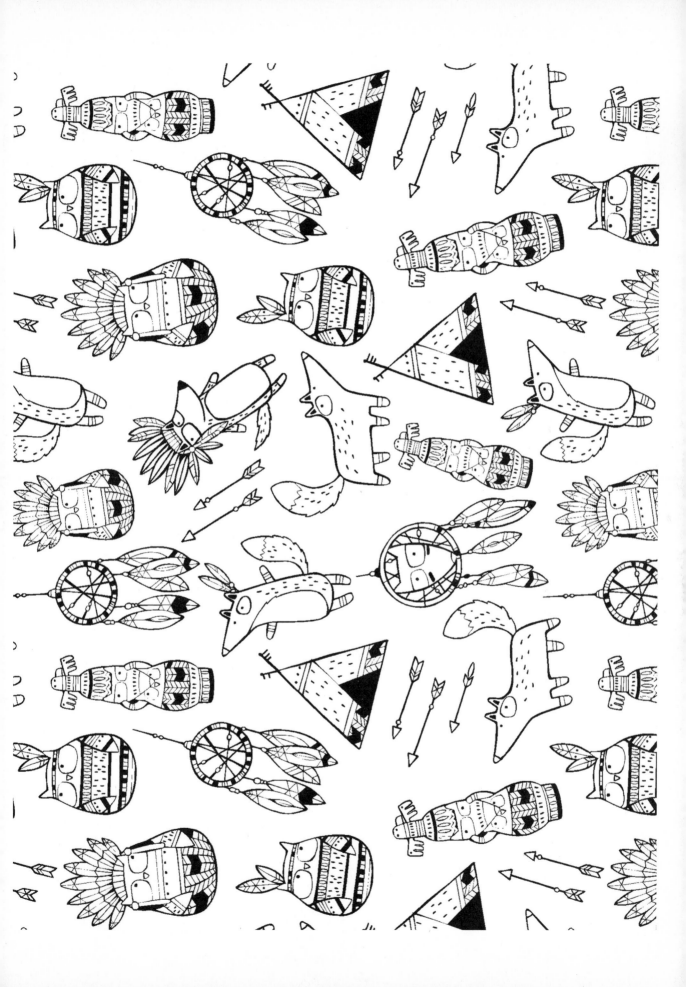

THE LITTLE THINGS I LOVE

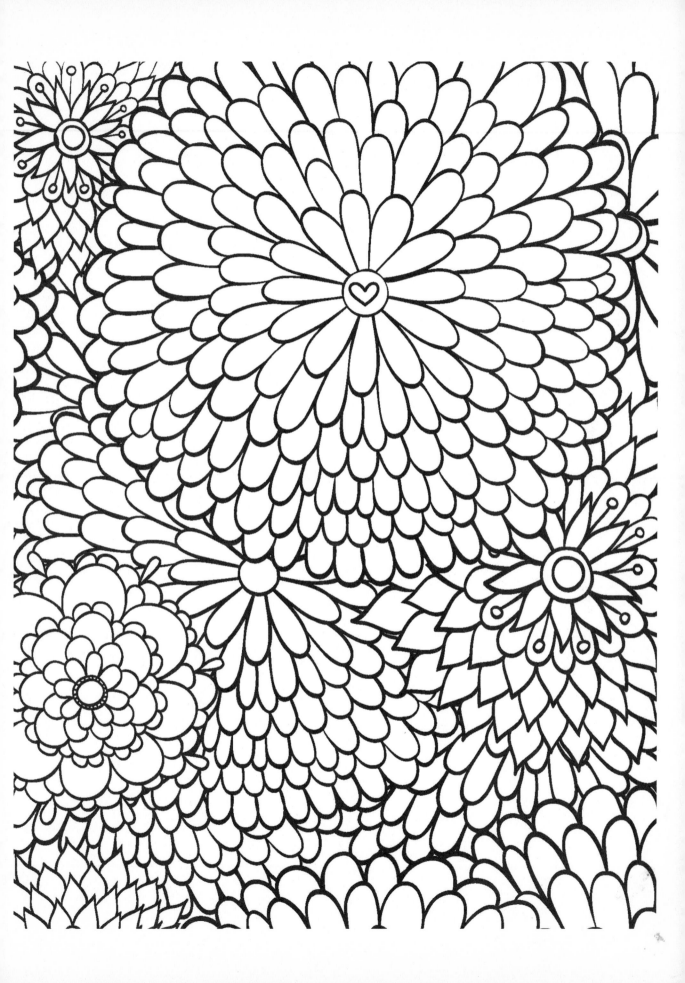

10 MOMENTS THAT INSPIRED ME

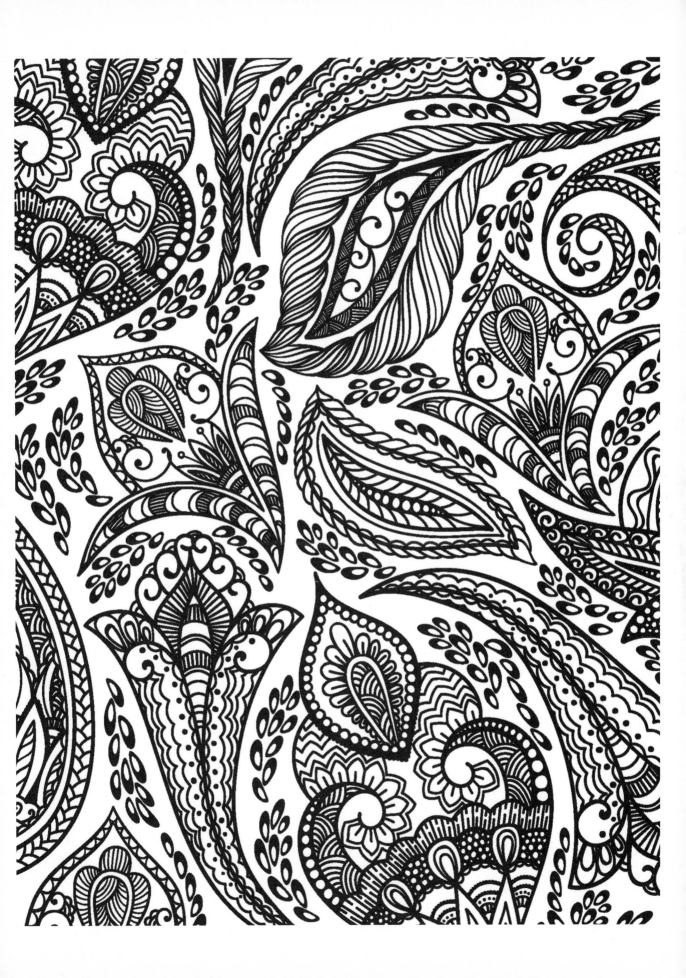

LAST NIGHT'S DREAMS, TOMORROW'S GOALS

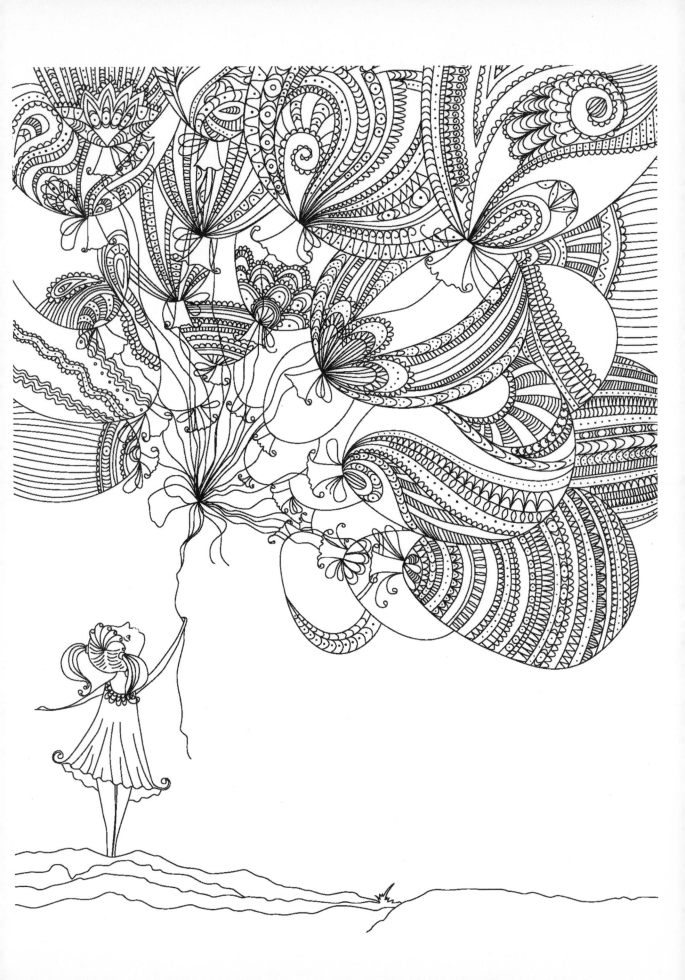

MY "LET GO" LIST

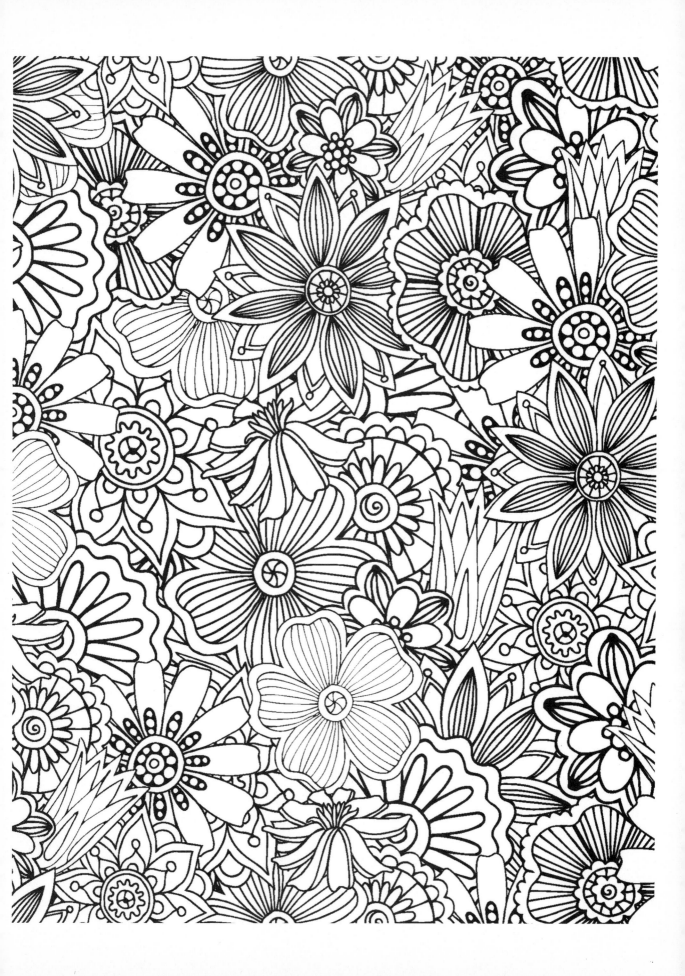

WORDS THAT BEST REPRESENT ME

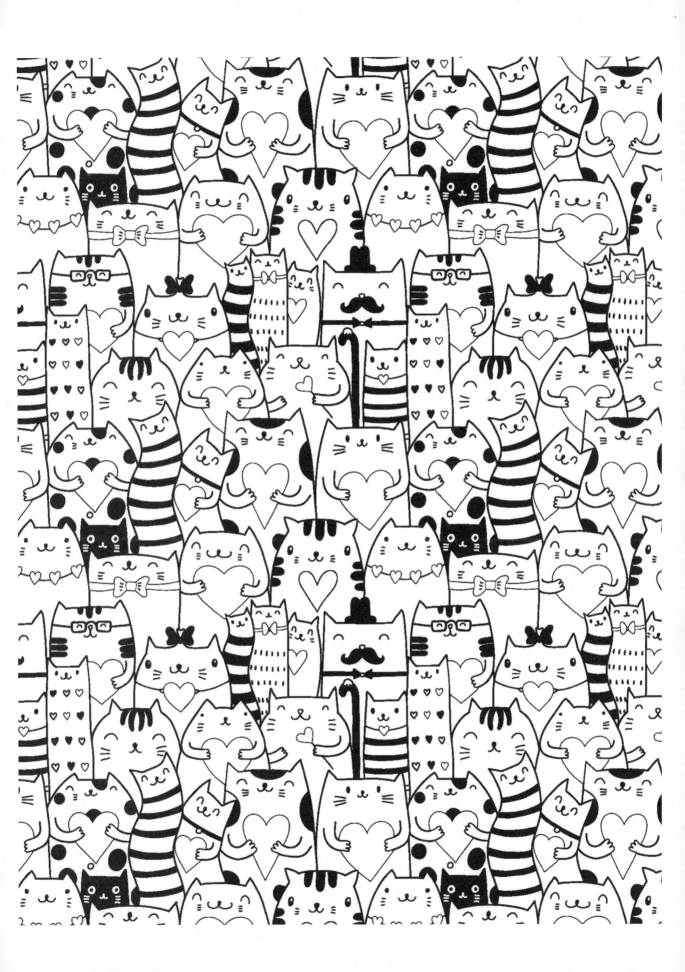

THE PEOPLE (& PETS!) I CHERISH

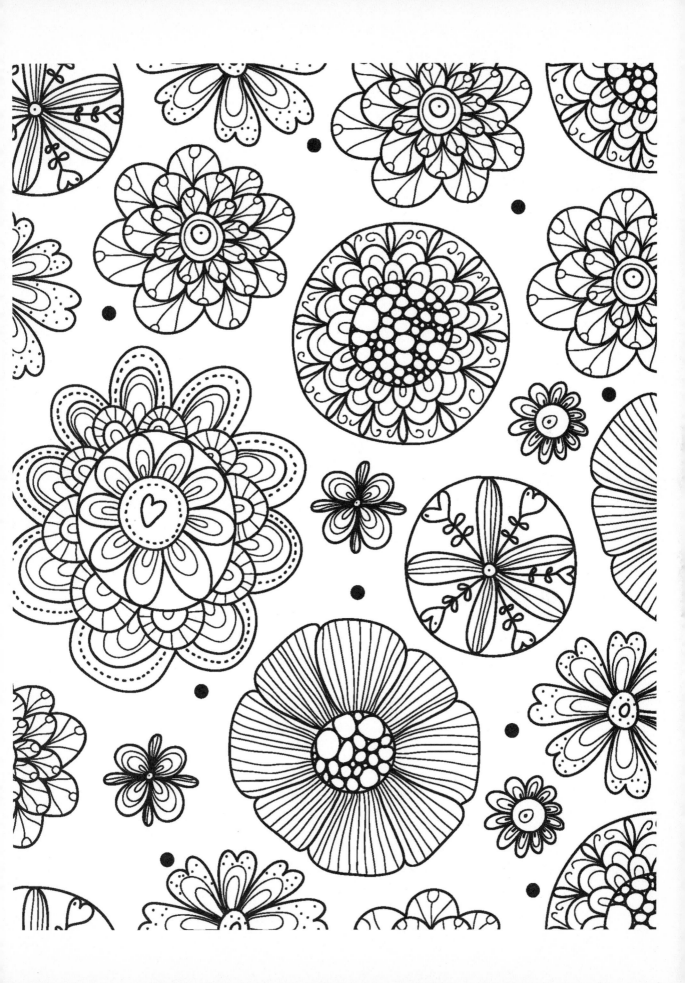

I AM HAPPIEST WHEN...

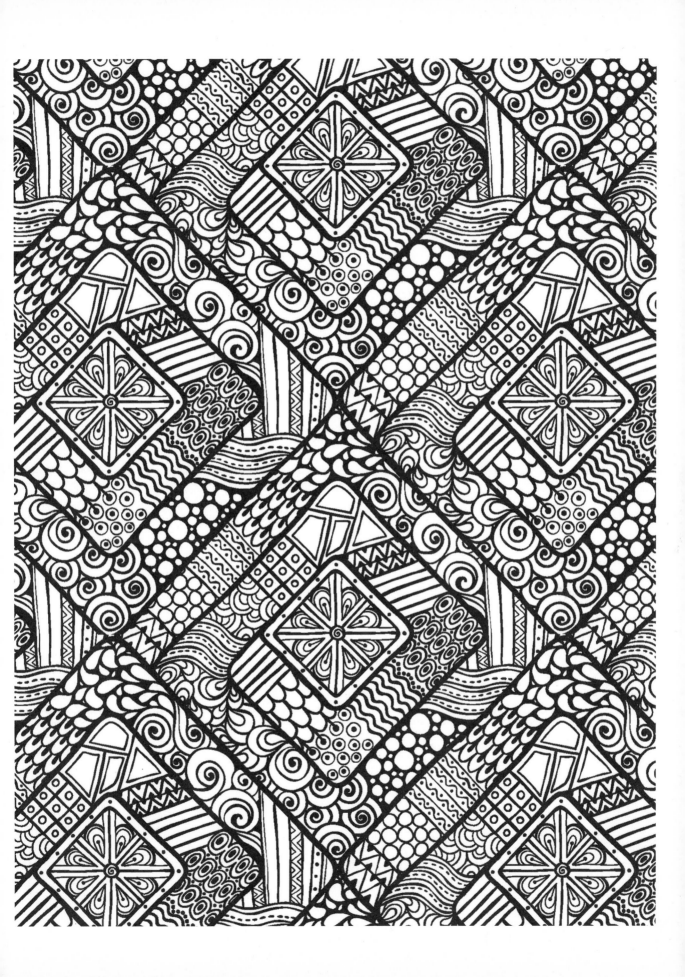

OH, THE PLACES I WILL GO...

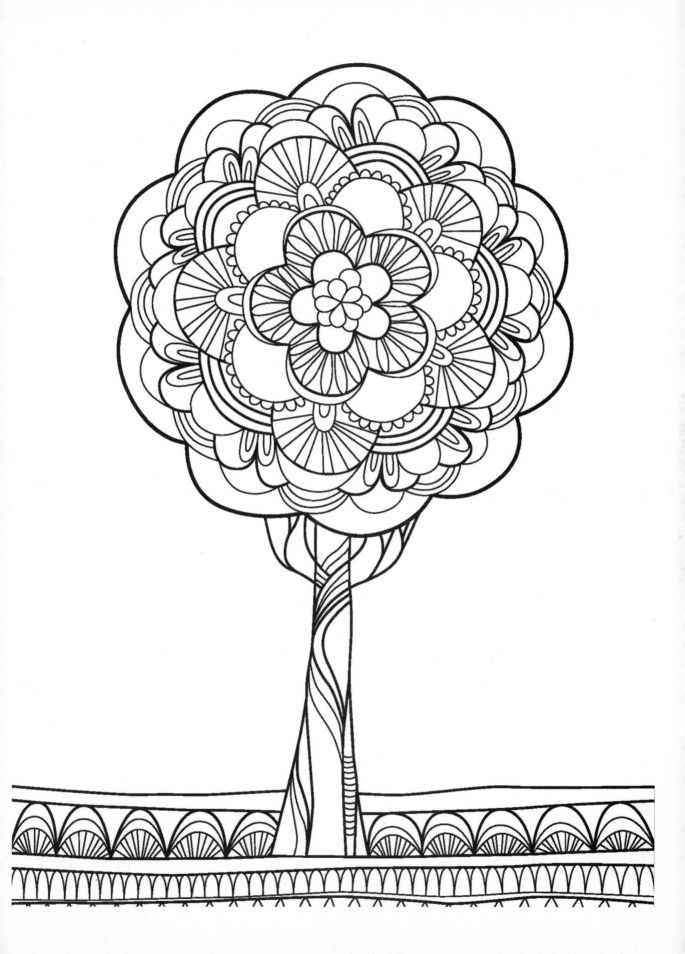

WHAT KEEPS ME GROUNDED?

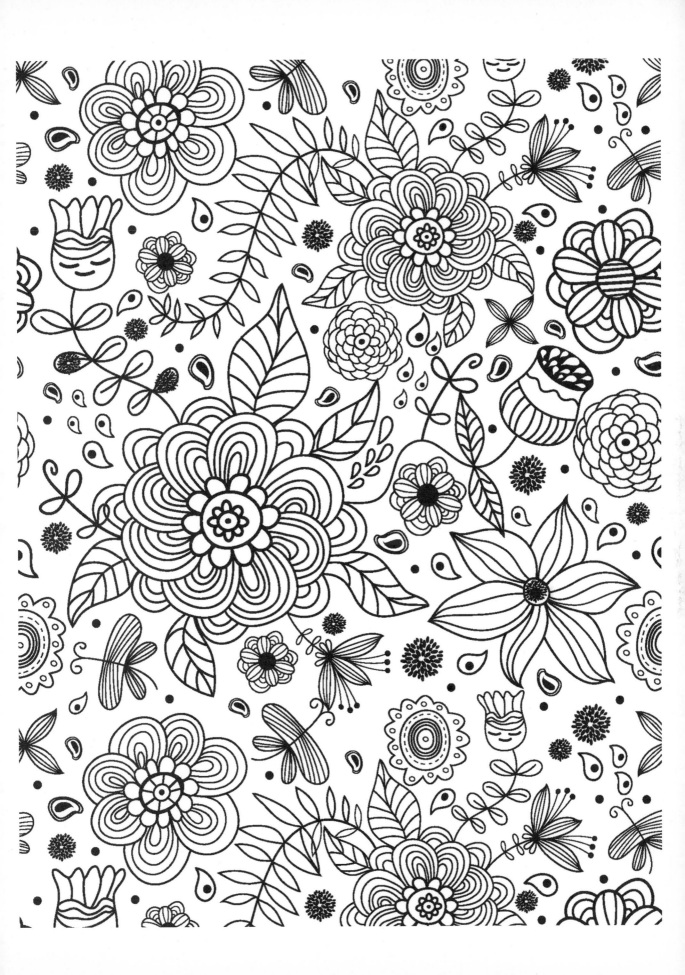

YOU GROW, GIRL!

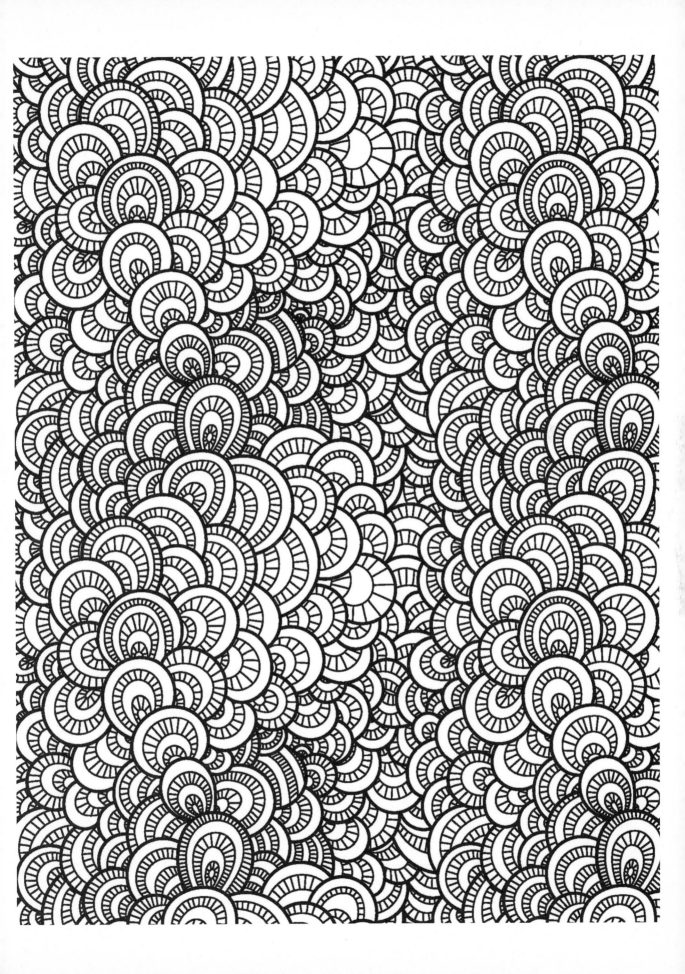

I CREATE MY OWN CALM BY...

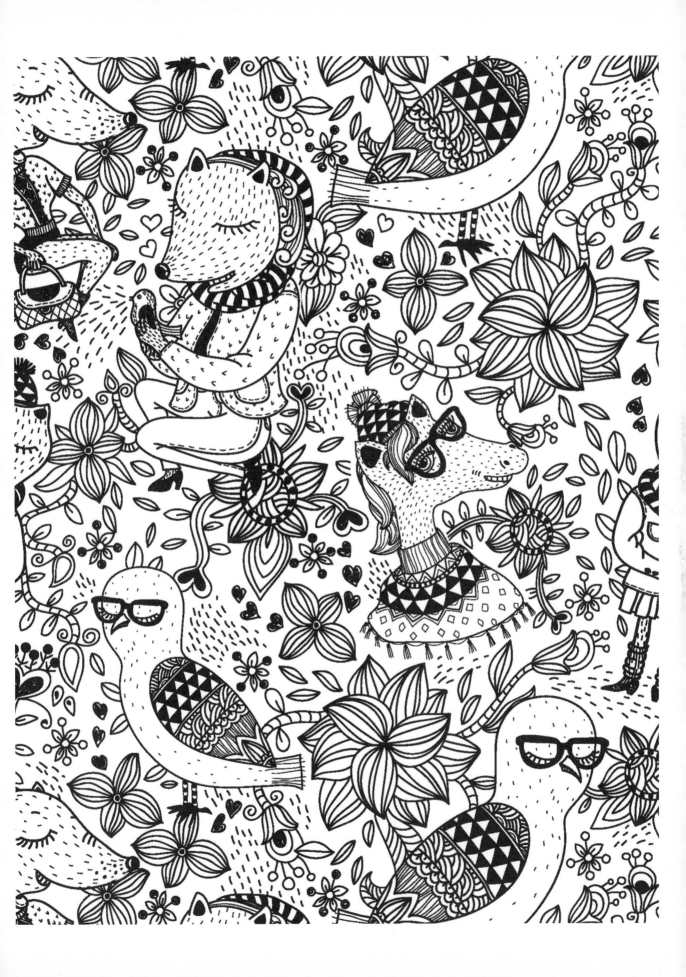

MY MOMENTS COLLECTION

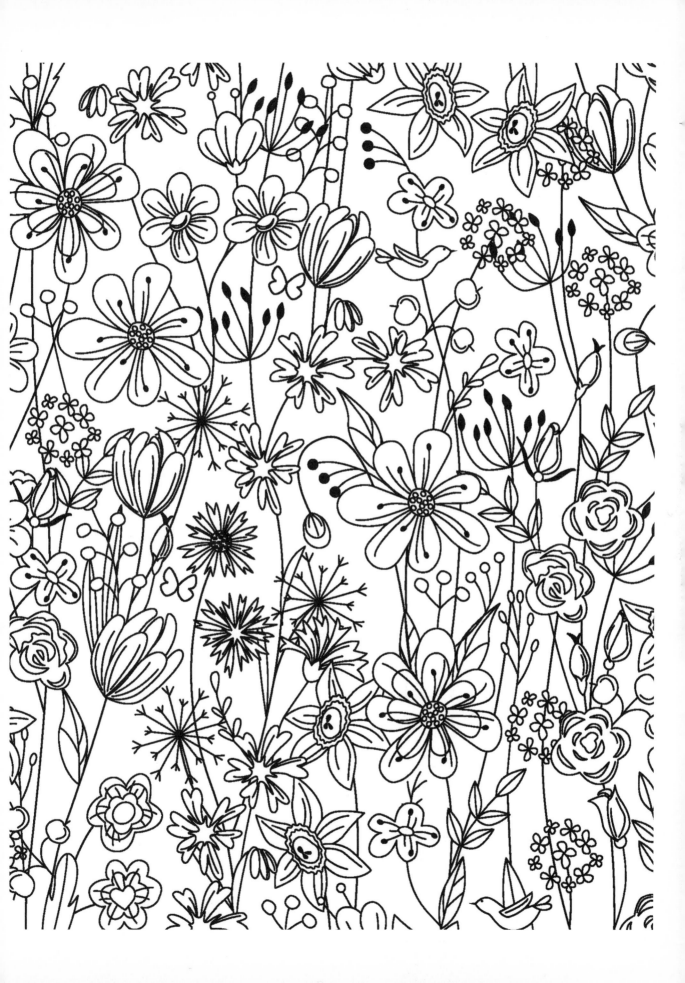

I FIND PEACE AND COMFORT IN...

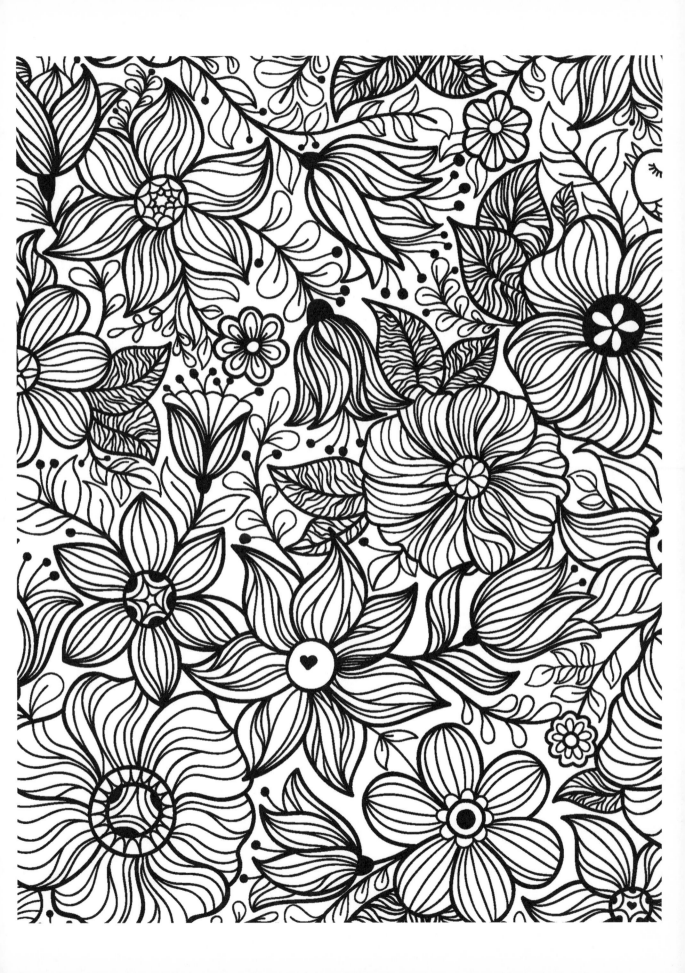

THE WISHES I CARRY

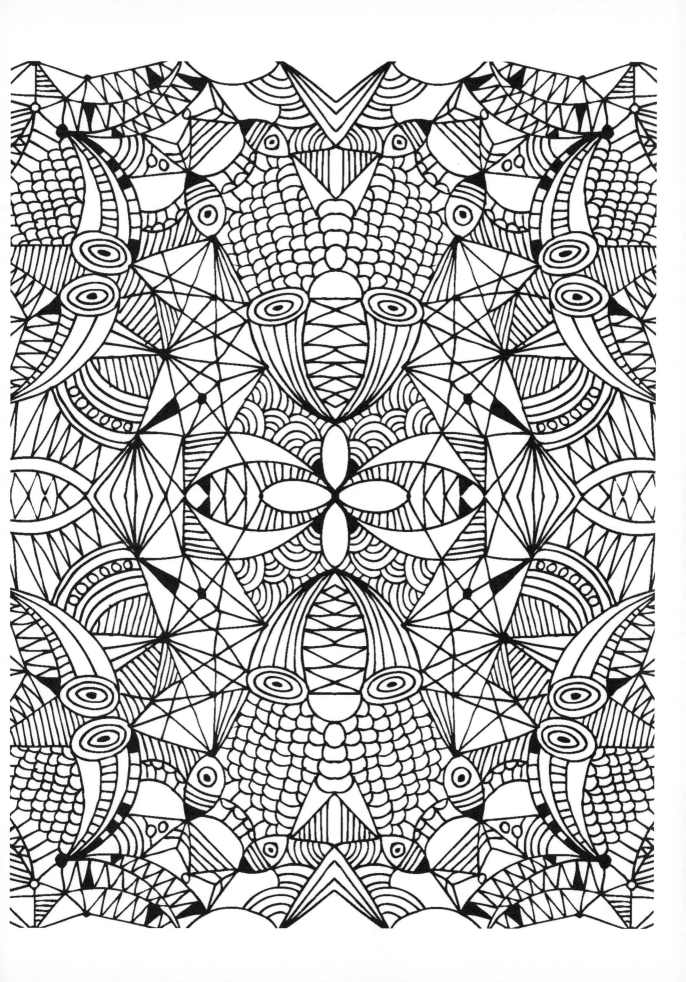

MY ADVENTURE SCHEDULE

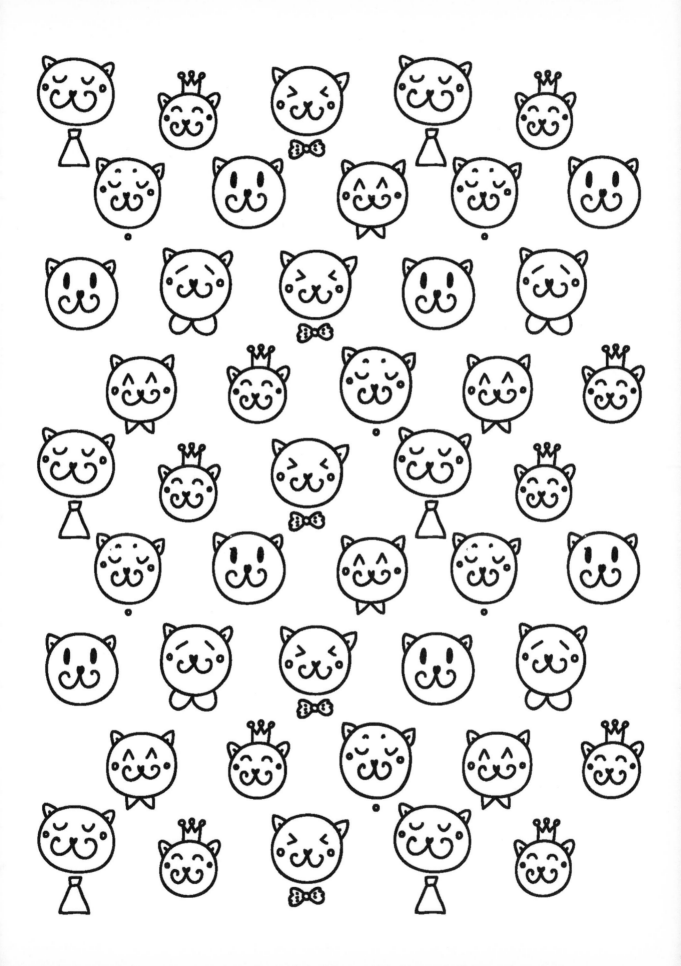

10 REASONS TO SMILE

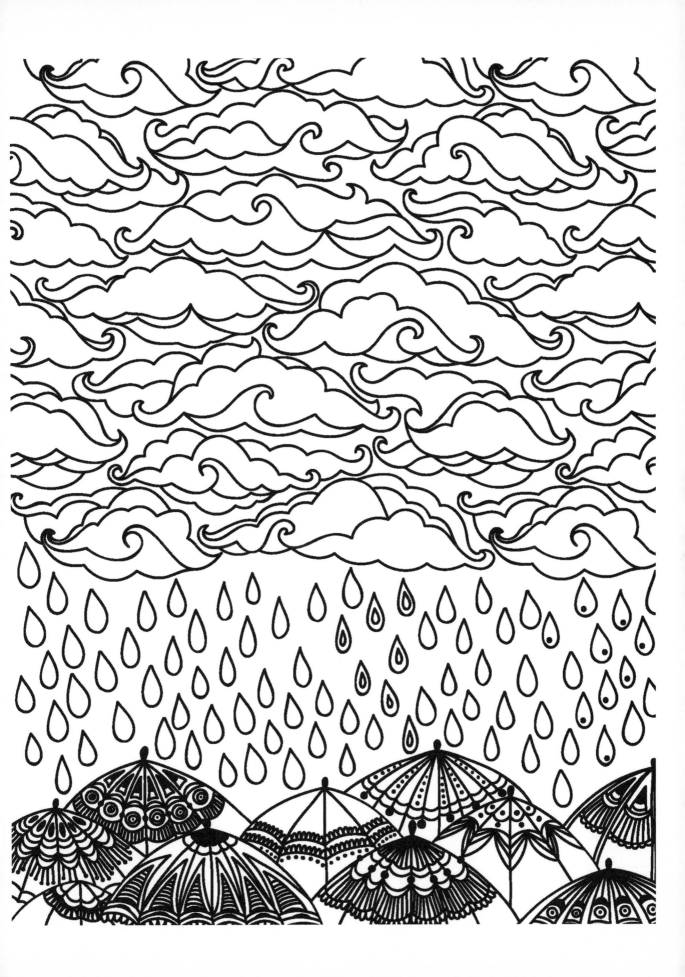

RAINY DAY THOUGHTS

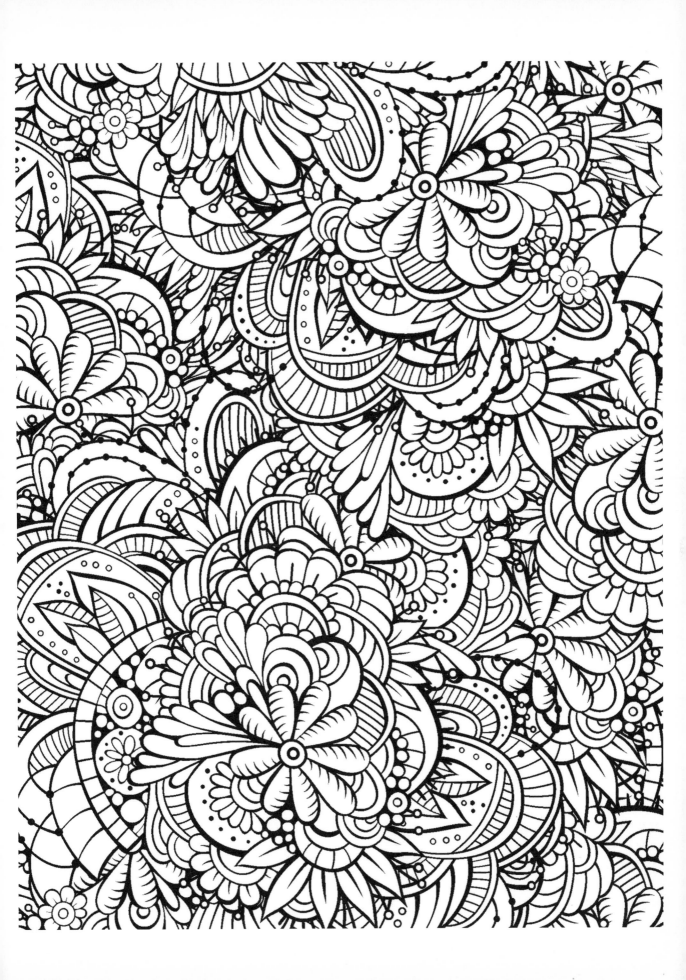

YOU'RE NEVER TOO OLD TO...

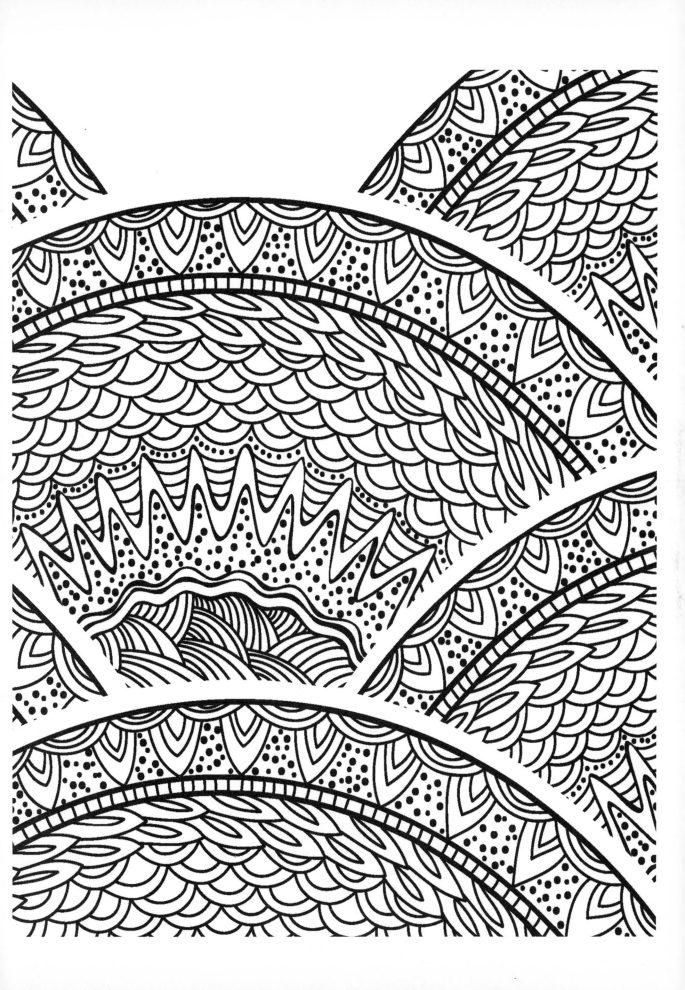

MY FAVORITE THINGS ABOUT ME

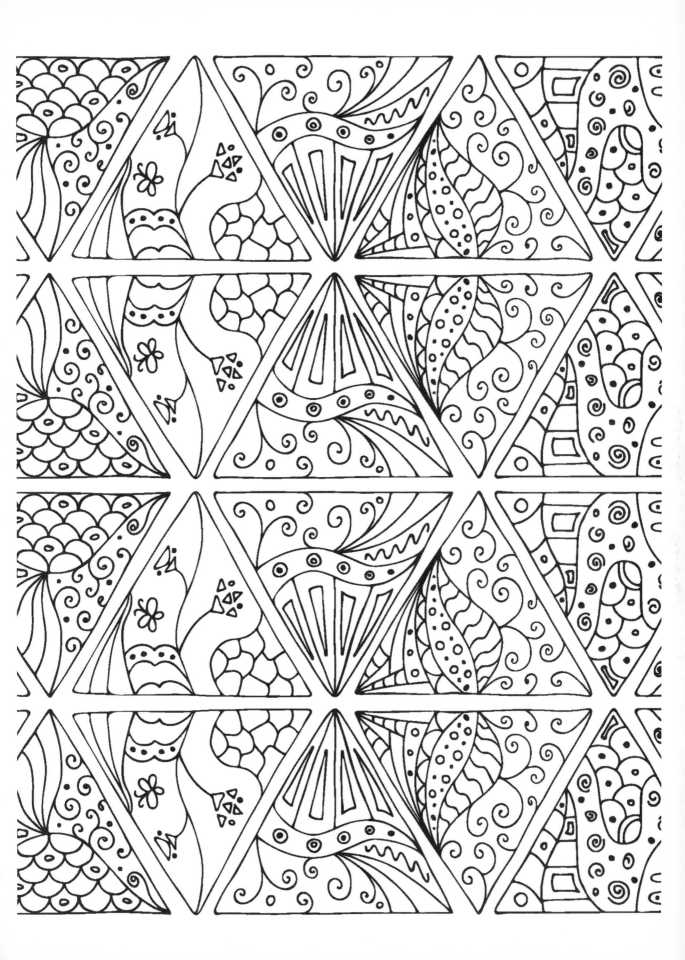

DARE TO COLOR OUTSIDE THE LINES BY...

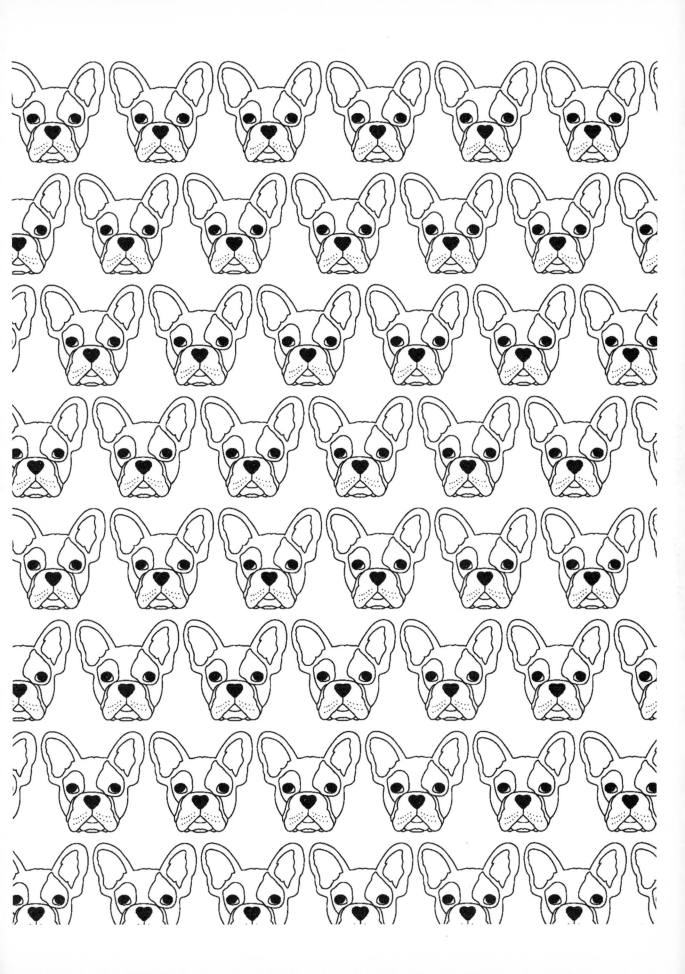

TODAY IS THE DAY I START...

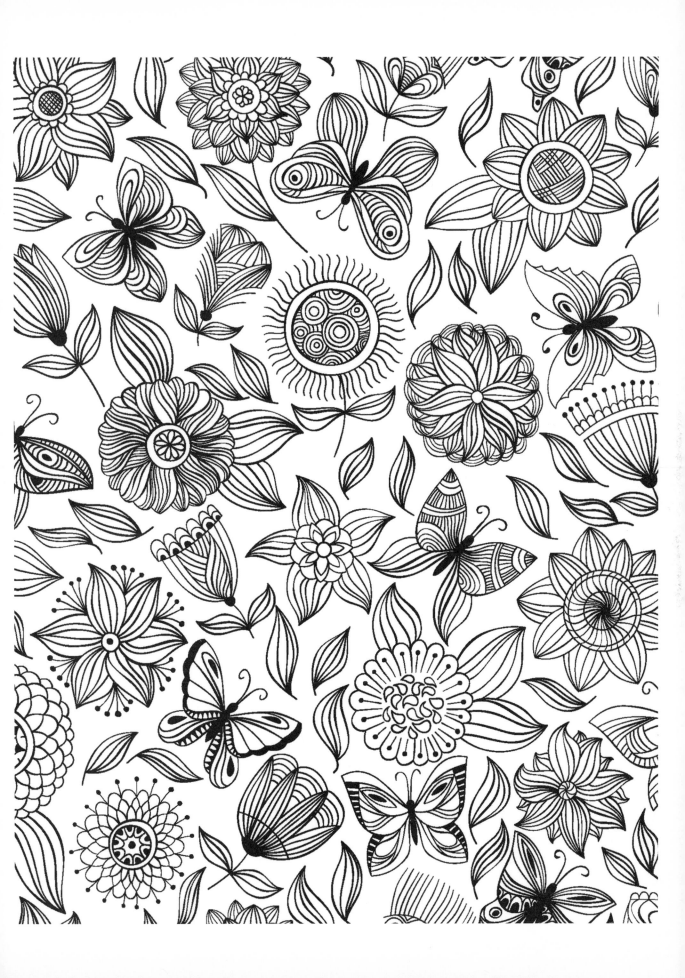

WHISPERS & SECRETS

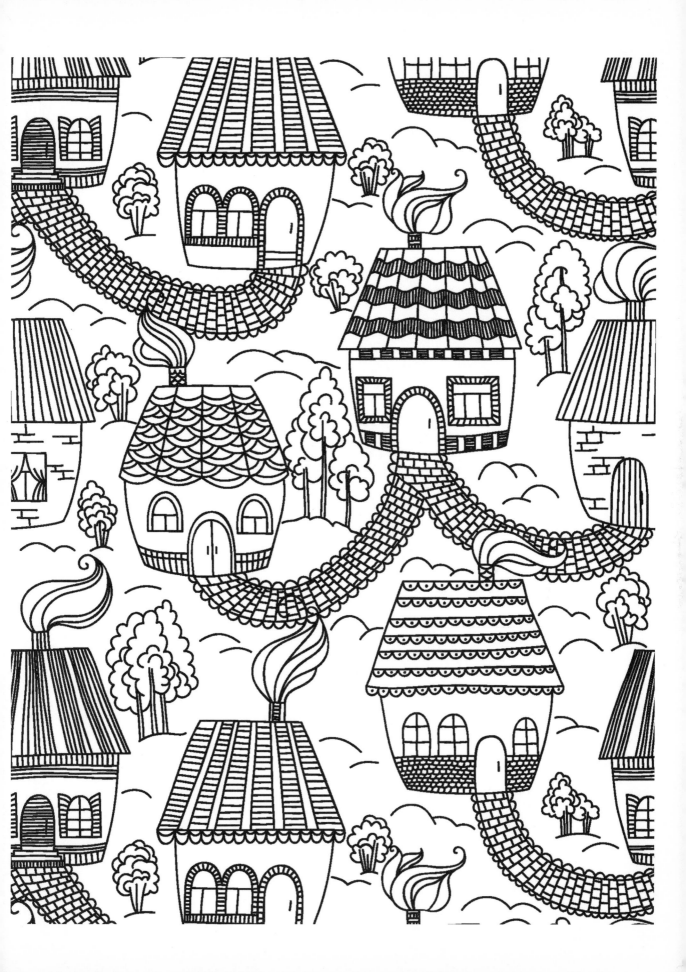

10 things that feel like home

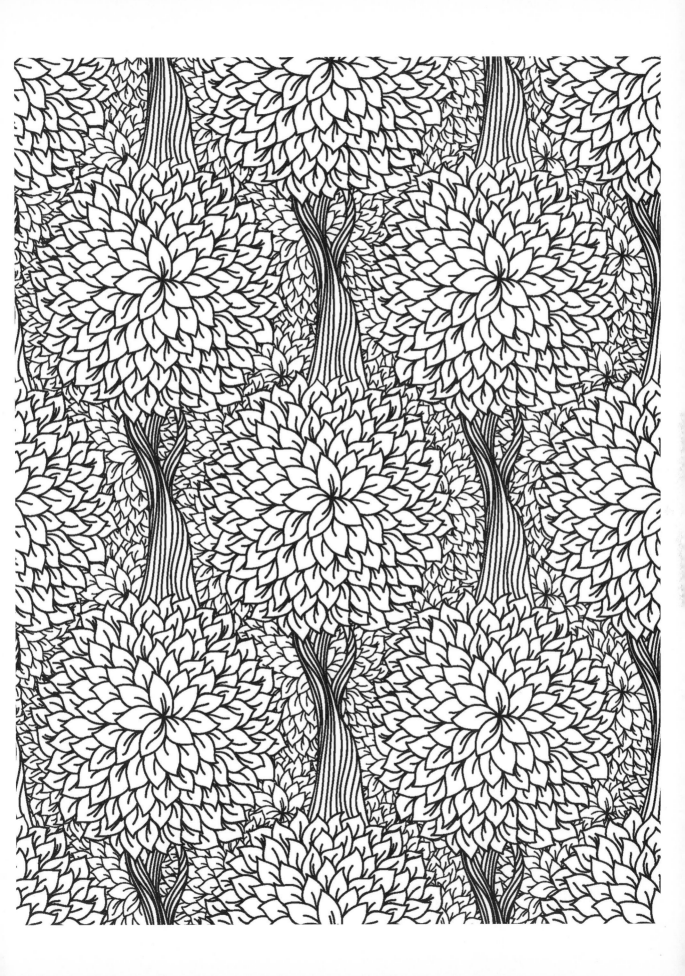

I DO MY BEST THINKING WHEN...

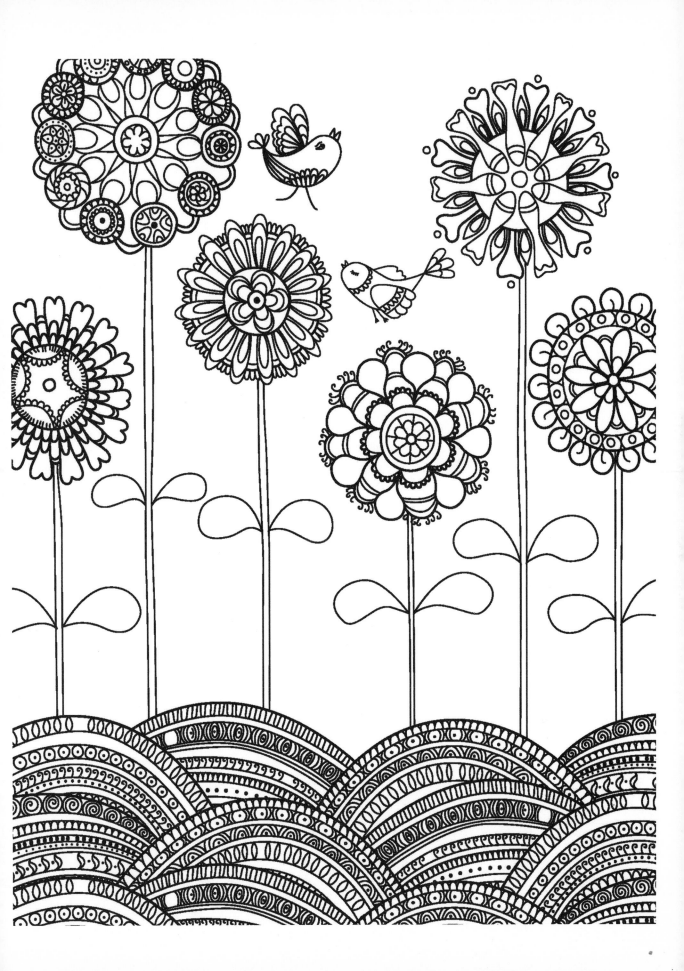

MY HAPPINESS STEMS FROM...

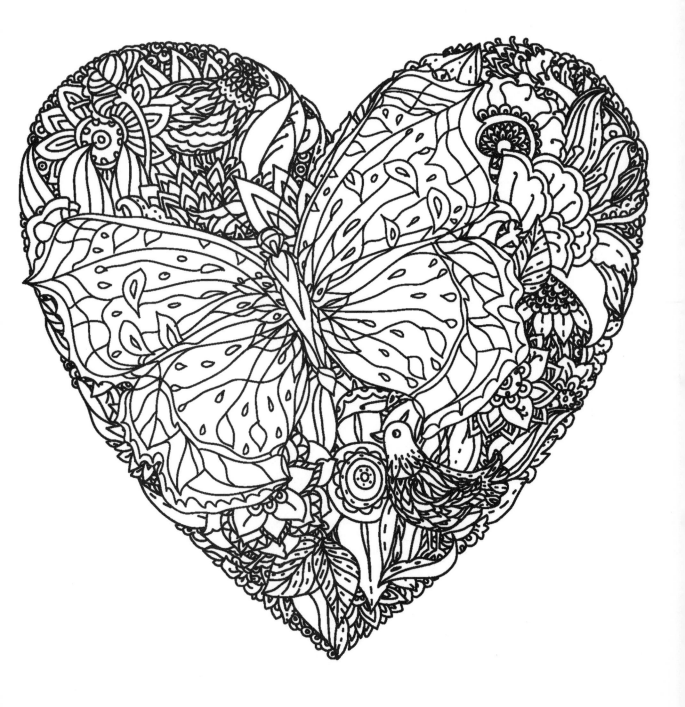

WHAT LOVE MEANS TO ME

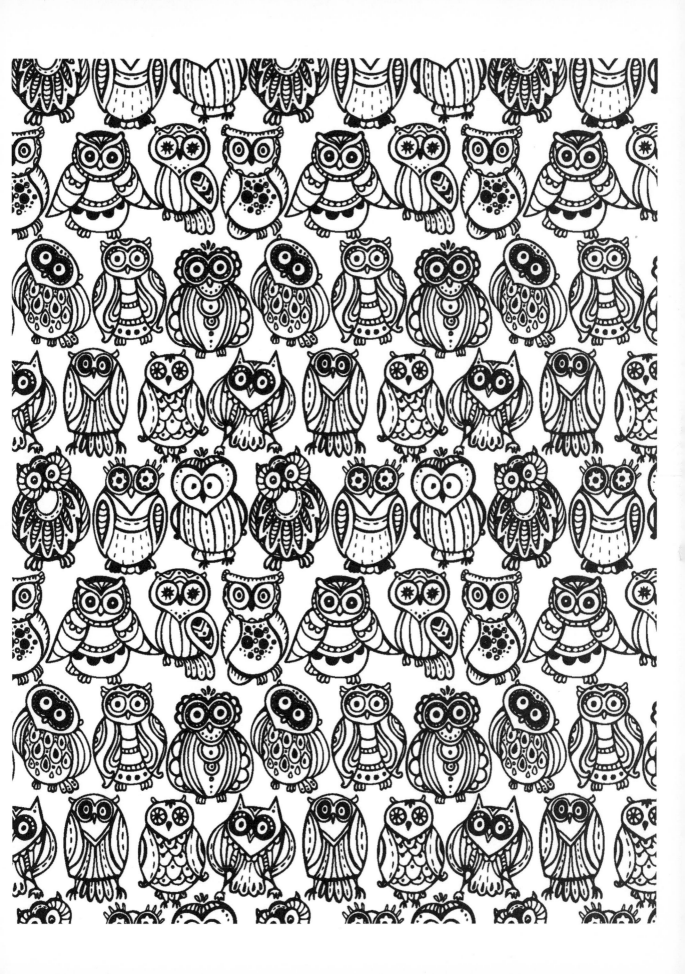

MY WHO'S WHO LIST

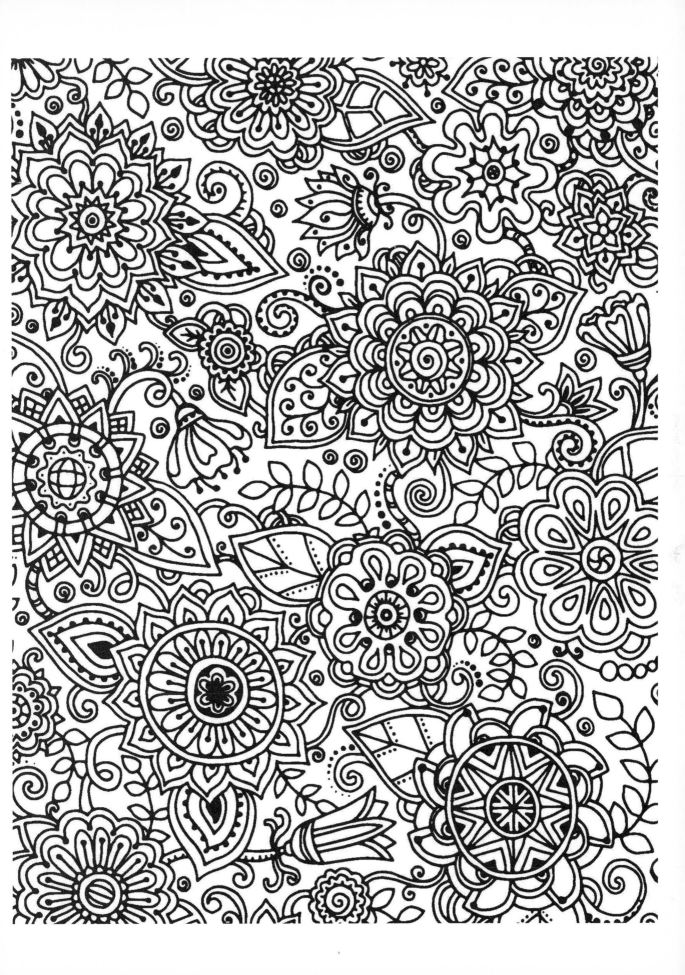

PASSION PROJECTS

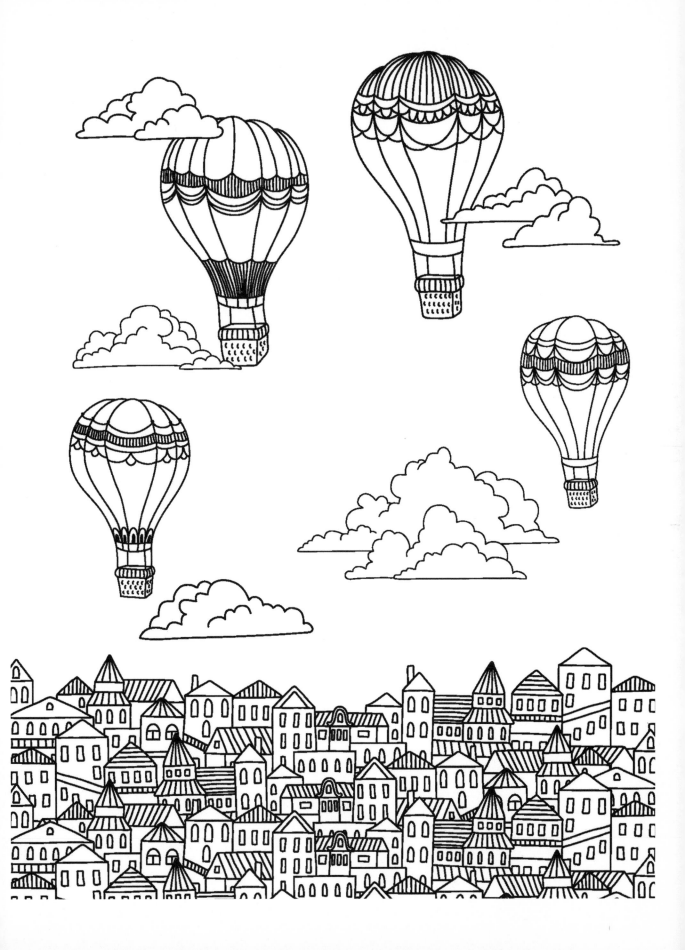

HEAD IN THE CLOUDS, FEET ON THE GROUND

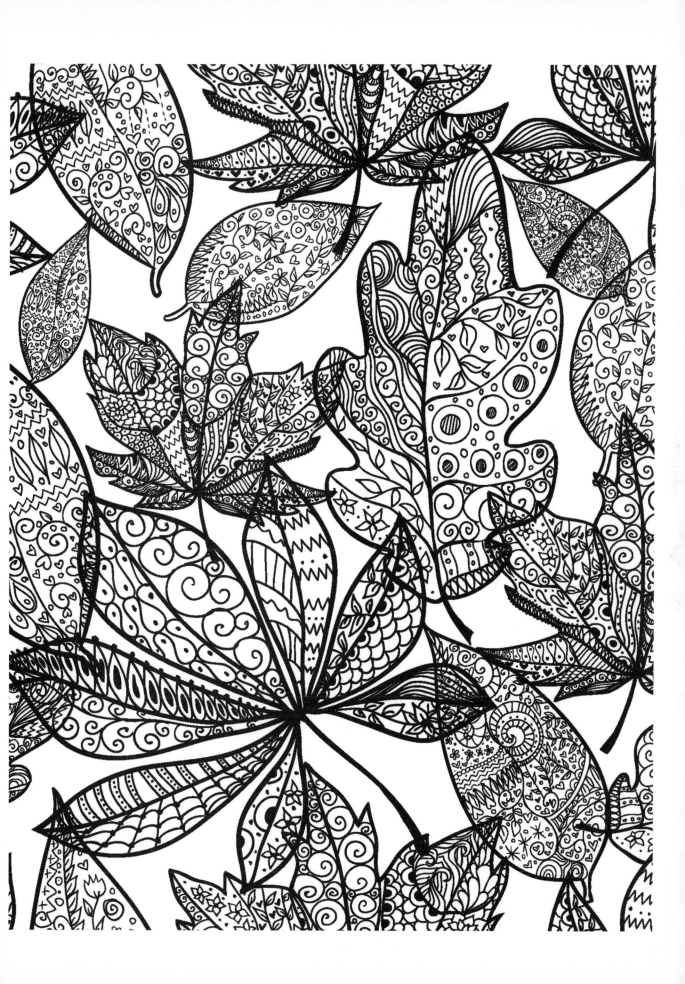

SEASONS OF CHANGE, JOURNEYS OF GROWTH

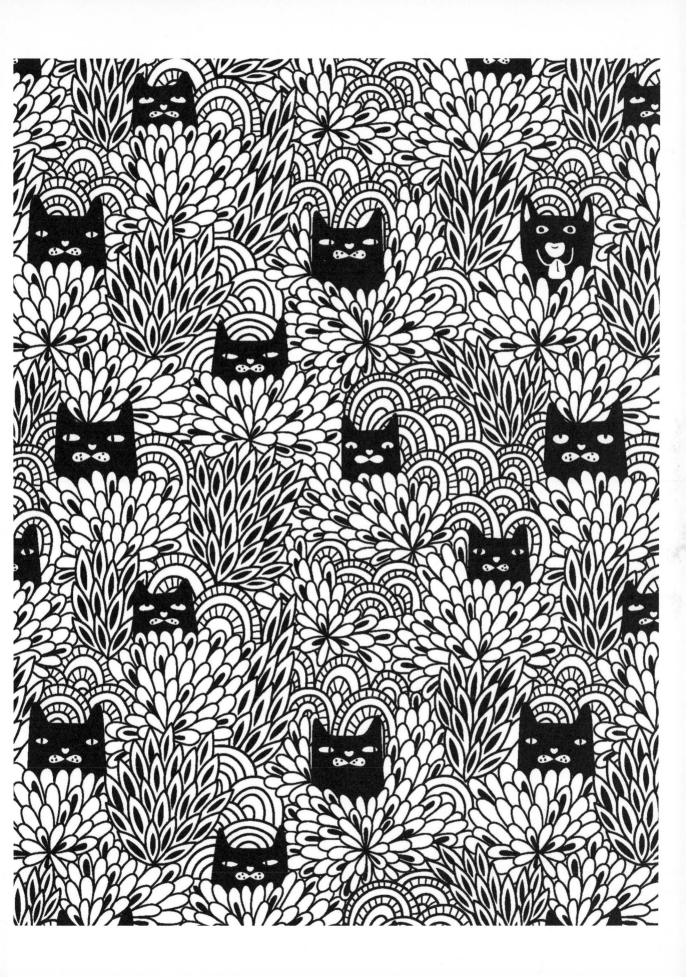

10 THINGS I WANT TO LEARN

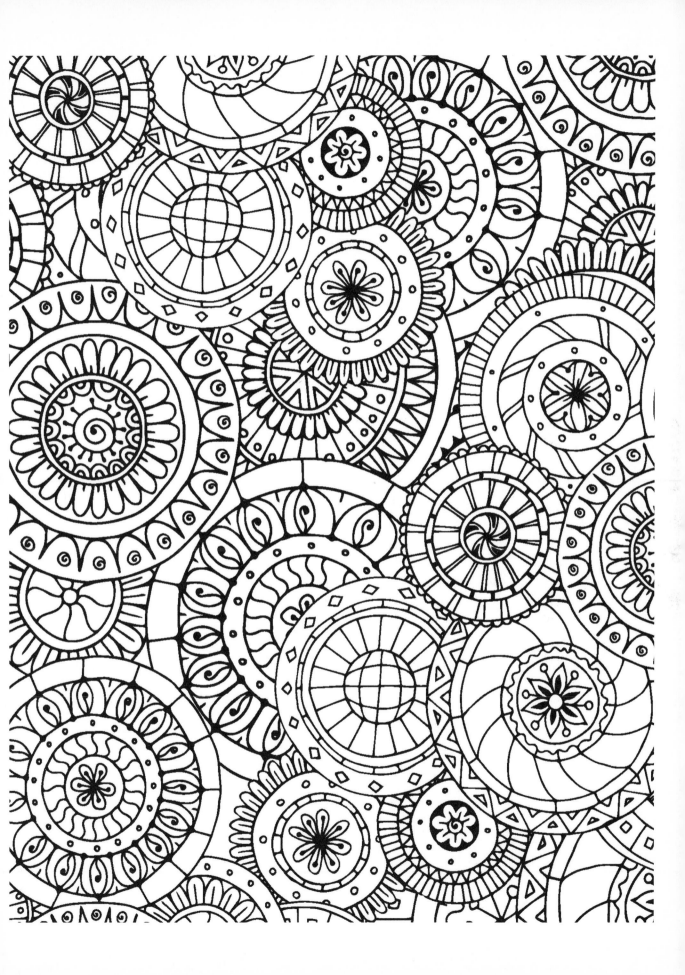

MY "CAN-DO" COLLECTION

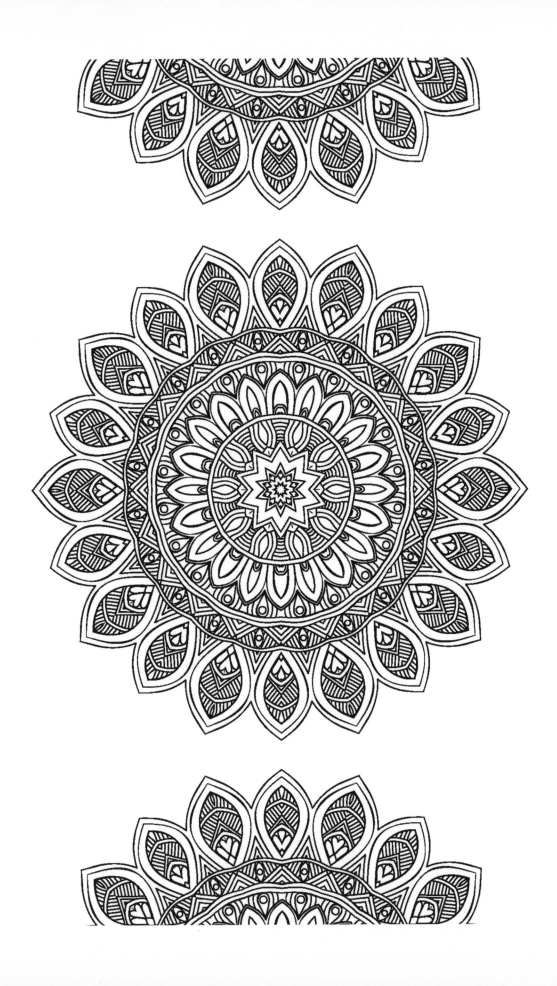

THE SUNNY SIDE OF LIFE

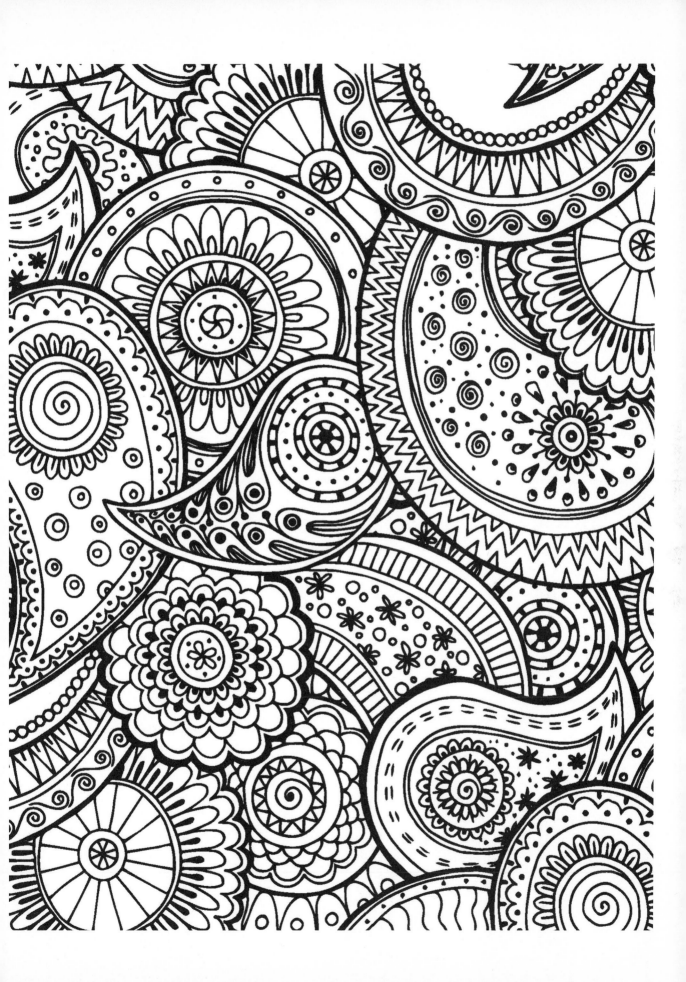

SIGNS IT'S TIME TO...

MY FAMILY (& FRIENDS) TREE

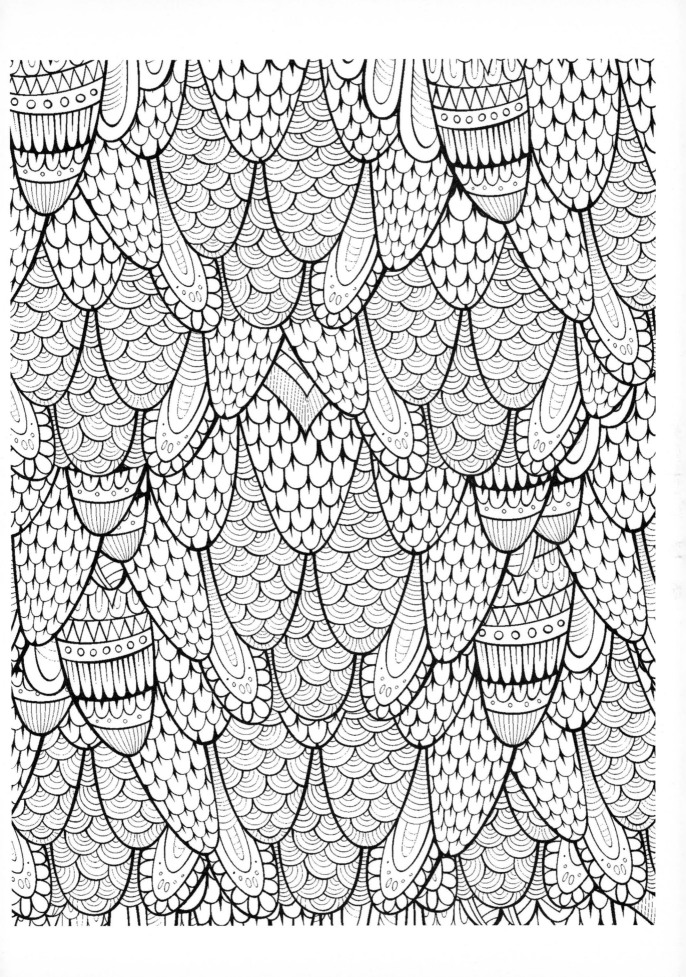

POEMS, RIDDLES & DOODLES

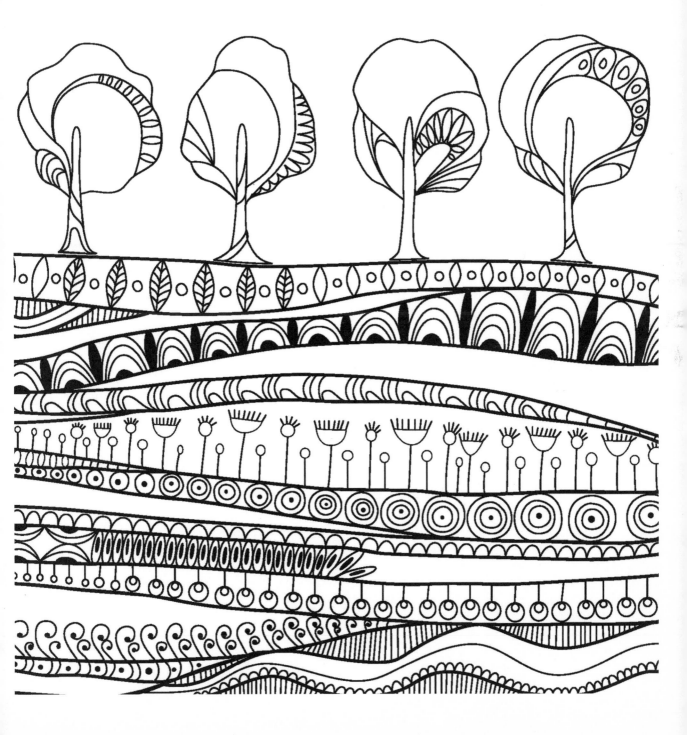

I FEEL MOST CONNECTED TO...

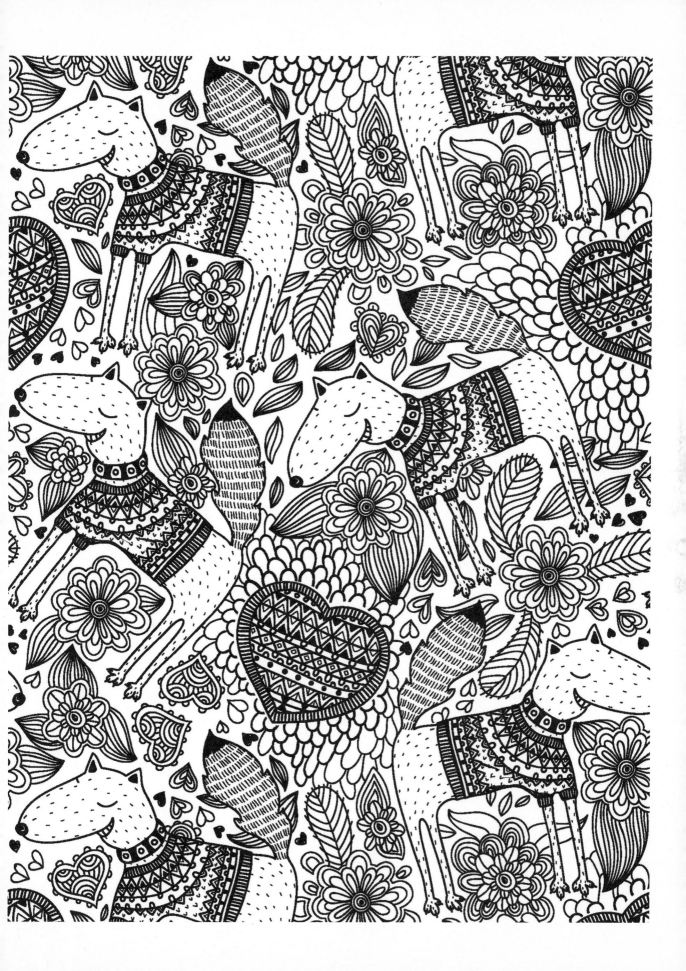

10 WAYS TO SURRENDER TO SILLY

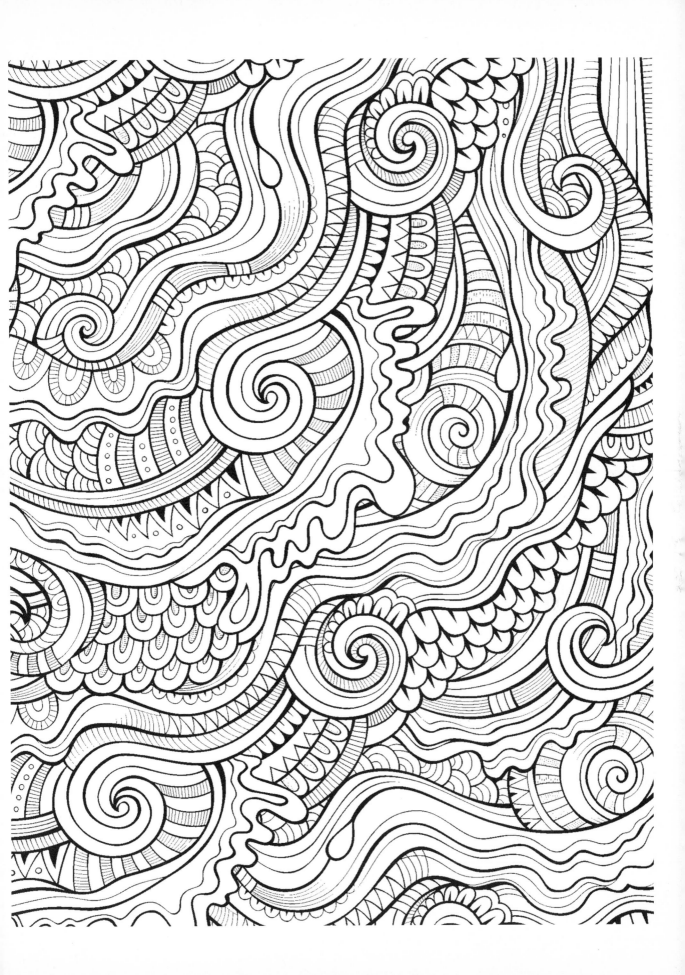

MY CREATIVE WAVE GUIDES ME TO...

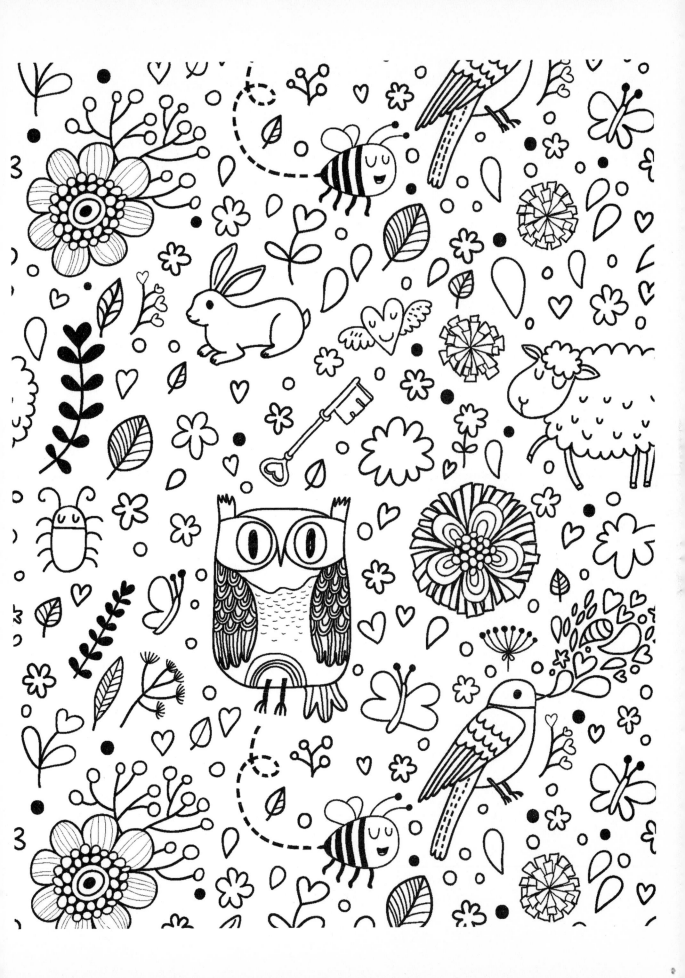

TREASURED KEEPSAKES AND MEMORIES

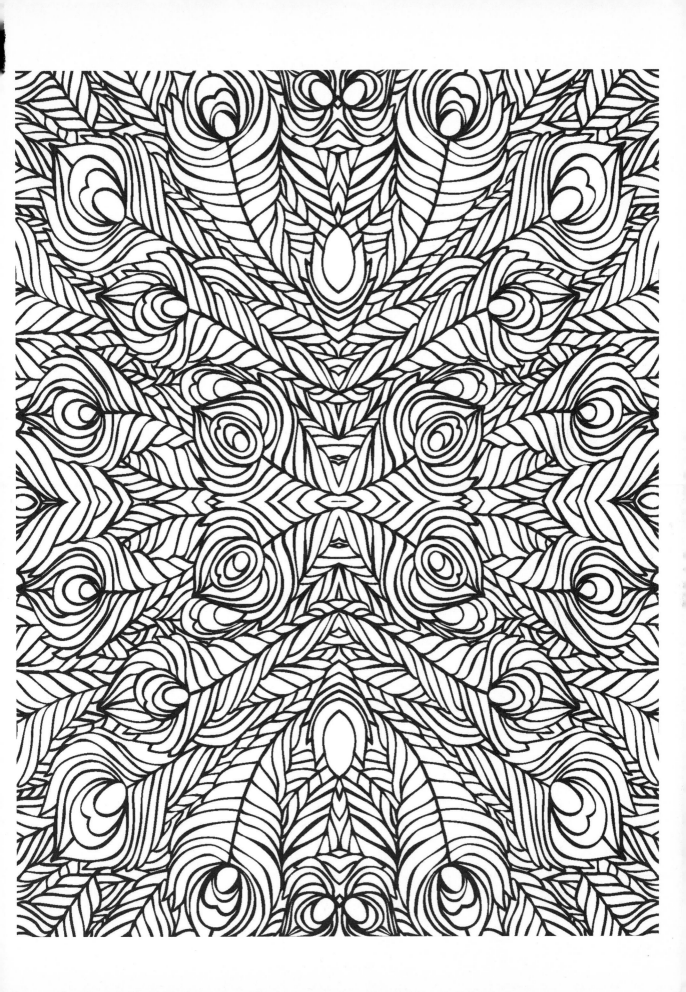

MAKE YOUR STORY LAST...